The Red Jacket

By Bill Morris

○ ☾ ☆
New ○ Sun Publications
Half Moon Bay, California

The Red Jacket Copyright © 2012 by New Sun Publications. Printed in the United Sates of America. No part of this book may be used or reproduced in any manner whatsoever without written permission except in the case of brief quotations embodied in critical articles and reviews.

For information contact:

Email: newsunpub@aol.com

New Sun Publications

227 Granelli Ave

Half Moon Bay, CA 94019

"To Claire, and, of course, to Kearney."

Preface

Sometimes we need to look back to remember who we are. Yes, that can be painful. You know this. And upon your mom's death a year ago, when you were just fifteen, I know you'll need to look back and remember her later on, years from now, when you need to find yourself again.

So I wrote a book about your mother. So maybe, years from now, you can remember a little more clearly who she was, who you were, what you had, where you come from. Because many parts of your mom, parts of me, are also parts of you. And you'll need to know about them to get you through.

Sometimes you and I don't have much to say. We know each other, we don't need to say much. And we have our own worlds we live in. You, yours, with your determination, goals, courage, and pride. Me with my wondering and looking for the right visions.

When we have nothing to say, it's not that we've said it all. It's because we have too much to say. And the things unsaid are carrying us forward, moving us along like separate twigs down a stream, each turning in our own current. We are moving on.

You are moving on. And, yes, as you get ready to leave the house you grew up in, we're separating. Distances are growing. Our lives becoming like two soap bubbles attached side by side, floating, but for just a bit more. So I wrote this book to keep us together a little longer. Later in your life.

Your Dad

The Red Jacket

Content

1	Your Mother's Name
2	Your Mother's Childhood
6	About Being Smart
9	A First Look
10	As a Baby
11	A Small Beautiful Thing
11	Cooking
13	The Gift of Dancing
16	The Color Wheel
18	A Little Lesson
19	A White Mustang
20	Hawaii
21	Moments in Oz
22	The Camolis
23	The Red Jacket
24	Opportunities and Misunderstandings
25	A Short History

33 A Small Thing Remembered Long
34 The Piñata
36 When You Were Born
38 Her Piano
39 Smaller Than a Bread Box
40 A Horror Tale
41 Pup
42 The Snail
43 Halloween Mother
44 Eating Together
45 Decorating the Tree
46 Titles
46 Questions for Someday
47 Being on Top of Things
48 Things We Won't Know
49 Years From Now
50 The Sun
51 A Detail
51 The Picture of Your Mother
52 Your Name

54 An Admirable Thing About the Rietmanns
56 Today You Cried
57 Compassion
58 Notebooks
59 Couscous
61 Tarot Cards
62 Makeup
63 Church
64 Gifts
65 Never Cried
65 The Art of Conversation
66 The Look
68 Ready to Serve

The Red Jacket

Your Mother's Name

Your mother had a beautiful first name: Kearney. To me it was unique, enthusiastic, lively, and charming. People were never sure how to first pronounce it, whether it was for a male or female; but once learned, it was a lovely name. When we were in the Peace Corps in Morocco, people who didn't know us well would come to visit. Your mother was fun to talk to, people enjoyed being around her, so much so that we became known by some as the "Kearneys." And if I quietly faded into the background as people enjoyed your mother, it was fine with me, I enjoyed being there, too.

I found out early that the name Kearney was a family heirloom. She shared it with her aunt, Aunt Kearney, whom your mother liked. It was the last name of a renowned family ancestor, General Stephen Kearney, who distinguished himself in the Mexican war, and who later became "the Father of the American Calvary." Even today there are streets in Colorado and forts that have your mother's name. And if there was glory

The Red Jacket

in that, I guess there was also some infamy for what was done in the West against our Native Americans. (And I'm told somewhere in the 1400s there was a knight with my last name who likely raised a sword against soldiers and peasants, so there's no telling what will come at you out of history in your own name.) So be prepared to make your own history, give it a better name, if you can. By your actions, make your name your own, like your mother's, make that name mean the good things about you. Kearney was a great name. You can make Claire mean great things to other people, too.

And to this day, I enjoy saying your mother's name: Kearney. And if the brightness of her name often eclipsed my own, I was fine with that. I never minded.

Your Mother's Childhood

I know just a little of your mother's childhood. I see it sometimes when I come across old photos: There stands a three- or four-year-old in a page-boy cut, squinting, one eye-brow raised to look at the camera, looking just a little concerned. A bit confused by something. A child holding the question why? She is not smiling and waving, as you and I knew her. Rather, she stands, no more than three feet tall, in a dress that bells out round her knees, as she waits beside her mother who is sparkling in a Sunday dress, gloves, and a little slanted hat. And beside her own mother smiling in lipstick, your mom stands as if beside a candle in church, quiet and watching.

Kearney's father, David, was an awkward man with a dry sense of humor. He grew up on a farm, went to college, went to war as air navigator, came home and started two successful shoe stores. "David's Shoes." He would have been the source of much kindness and love, excepting family life was bound by the strict do's and don'ts of the 1950s. He was seen, perhaps kept at a distance, by a family inner circle that would hear a joke from him and reply with an "Oh, David."

Kearney's mom had grown up on a farm around horses. She went to college and became a nurse. She was, I think, looking for the propriety of suburban life, the 50s household parties and the success of store-owning retailers. They were part of a country club, where Kearney spent some happy summer evenings at a crowded pool. They water-skiied in groups of families

The Red Jacket

related by business along The River. They were churchgoers and played in small-town Republican politics.

Here are snippets of her childhood. When Kearney was just a toddler, barely with words, she was alone in a bedroom with a relative's small baby. The baby rolled off the bed. And as relatives came in, someone asked Kearney sternly, accusingly, what happened to the baby. Little Kearney struggled to explain, saying only, "It fell on the ceiling,"—so young she even mixed up "ceiling" and "floor." She was accused, treated caustically for saying something nonsensical, "ceiling!" She remembered the puzzling injustice of that her entire life. Think of it, adults who had left a baby unsupervised and blaming a child.

And I remember Kearney telling me how she would put her sister Kris to bed, floating sheets and blankets down on her in "the waterfall." And late at night, Kearney would wake up in the dark, completely afraid. Needing to go to the bathroom. But waiting and waiting, until desperate, she tiptoed down the hallway to the toilet, terrified her father would shout out in his sleep, as he did each night, about his brother and being beaten on the farm. She spent hours in the dark, afraid,

The Red Jacket

waiting, to slip down the hallway to relieve herself, afraid of her father's haunted shouts.

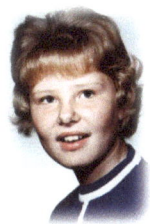

And older, now in junior high, your mother once got a new outfit, a beautiful emerald green skirt, jacket, and leggings. She was very pleased with these new clothes. And as she mounted the bus to go to school the first morning she wore it, someone yelled out, "Hey, Kearney's legs molded!" And that confused her, and hurt her, and made her feel bad about her outfit. So she couldn't wear it. And the cruelty of that, well, doesn't it make you want to cry? It makes me want to cry.

And your mother once told me something about her childhood that could change the world. She told me that as a small child, when her family went to church, she was taken away from her family and put in the church basement with the other kids. She stayed down, separated and apart from the church music and candles and singing up above. She knew the cold and bitterness of a child left behind by family, in an unexamined institution. And as an adult she wondered why.

The Red Jacket

And so, many years later, in your mother's church, she taught a wise and seeing priest to keep children as part of the church. Don't shelve them in the basement. Let them into the church hall, in the middle of the sermon with all their noise, and innocent questions, and let the sermon be to them. Let the adults sit and listen as the priest speaks to them. Make kids the center, and leave place for the family in church to grow. And this brought on a true rejuvenation of the church. Dozens of new families came in. Our little church grew with more and more families coming to a worship hall where children were welcomed, honored, and as respected as anyone else. Your mother's church and this fine priest made a new church that was light, and bright, and growing. True rejuvenation. A childhood lesson. And one way how your mother changed her world.

About Being Smart

People see life through their little lens. And smart people think their lens is a little clearer and sharper. And it's common that most use that lens to confirm their own superiority. And it becomes just another form of discrimination against others.

Your mother had exceptional intelligence, beyond what most "smart people" you might deal with could understand. This was often a source of pain for her.

The Red Jacket

She was quick-minded, read constantly, and knew her topics deeply. Such that other smart people approaching her never suspected that this person had deeper insights and farther-reaching thoughts than they. She spoke fluent French, without accent, as native speakers often admired and commented to me. She was exceptionally intuitive, such that upon first meeting people, knowing them briefly, she could tell you infallibly who was a secret drinker, who was a bull in a china shop wrecking all he touched, who would never finish his work. Over the years, I grew to know the truth of her insights and never questioned them. I knew she was smarter than me. I found I had to clean my own little lens.

And this is how her pain arrived. I watched it happen countless times. She was an editor par excellence. So good that the average "smart person" writer didn't suspect. As a magazine editor-in-chief, she would provide corrections and reworking of poorly written prose. And smart people balked, gave her frustrated arguments, because to them their work made perfect sense. She just didn't understand. And she would weather this furrowed-browed disbelief from her writer skeptics who couldn't believe their little lens wasn't superior and clear. They'd leave, upset. And inevitably, a day or so later, they'd come back and admit that your mom was right. It wasn't clear, it didn't say what they meant. They were wrong. And that was the beginning of a deeper respect for her that she earned. But it cost her arguments and pain. And I saw this happen over and over, as smart people came up with the same old "smart" answers, and hadn't gone beyond what smart people always say. And your mom, she received remonstrance and pain, until they caught up with her later.

But many many smart people of high acumen and good character grew to know your mother's insights and mind. You know the Church was absolutely full, people standing outside, the night of your mother's funeral—even though you and I invited only family. Hundreds of people came, and these were the people who knew her. You and I were astonished, somehow the town, so many people, had found out and we hadn't said a word.

And your mother's mind had always touched deeply on the topics that concerned her. She read hundreds of books on the Holocaust, psychology (all the works of Jung), on business, and at the end of her life on spirituality, love, and forgiveness. And I was always sad that she never wrote down her thoughts for us, for others. She was a scholar who learned all these things for herself. And all the insights she gave out to these "smart" people, she gave them out for free.

A First Look

When I first saw your mother, something happened. It's an old story. She was working behind the checkout desk of the university library and I was coming out of the stacks of Shakespeare. And as I put down my book on the counter and looked up at her, I saw something. There was something about her that took hold of me, a difference. Something about her, the wholesomeness of a Doris Day with a touch of Marilyn Monroe, made me stop. I saw she had a little gold locket, an Indian Om, on her chest, and I just had to ask her. "What's your name?"

The three fraternity rats behind me looked at each other and mocked nasally, "What's your name?"

And she was looking at me, too. We both recognized something. And that first look lasted for nearly 30 years.

The Red Jacket

As a Baby

Your mother was ever thoughtful of others. By thoughtful, I mean she thought about people and how they lived, and what made them the way they were.

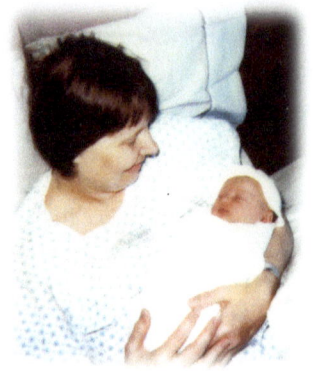

And when you were born, you had been deep in her thoughts. As the youngest, newest, wrinkly infant, you'd already been thought deeply about, and how your world would be. She wanted it to be a world that met your needs, that gave you no doubt you'd receive the things you needed just as you needed them. She believed if a baby cried, it was never in anger, never a reproach, a baby never punishes, a baby only cries its need. And babies have pretty simple needs, food, changing, holding, sleep, love. So, when you cried, we never left you crying, we always went to you and picked you up and supplied the need. Even when sometimes we were a little puzzled. We never let you cry yourself to sleep. If you cried in the night, she got up and made sure your needs were met. Because she wanted you to believe the world would be there for you, that life was abundant, that you would get by, that there was loving support near at hand, that the world was a good place to be. And when you cried for something. Well, help was coming. With your mother's thoughts and love behind it.

And that's the world she wanted you to live in.

(And I have to say it worked, it made you.)

A Small Beautiful Thing

Here's something you'll remember about your mother. A small beautiful thing.

Whenever Kearney saw me coming, saw you coming, saw someone she liked coming, she lit up and waved. It was a cheery and bright greeting, with her smile and a slanted headshake to show happiness.

I saw this so many times, it comes to mind instantly. A person sees you and waves because she likes you. She told you you were a good person from a hundred feet away.

Cooking

Your mother and I cooked completely differently. We both cooked according to our tastes. Both feeding you according to

The Red Jacket

our own palates. But cooking was different for Kearney than for me.

When Kearney made a dish, a couscous or harira that we learned to make in Morocco, she was precise and measured the ingredients. I remember her sprinkling in salt as if it were precious pixie-dust grain by grain between her rubbing thumb and forefinger. There were precise 1/4 teaspoon amounts laid into bubbling liquids. Dry things and wet things were mixed in the proper order, a recipe was used and read. The oven preheated.

As you know with me, it's different. It's all chemistry, and how you get the chemicals in doesn't make much difference. If the boiling water needs salt, I throw in enough to make a splash. Add garlic powder, pepper, Worcestershire sauce until there's some taste. And lately always a dab of butter. (Excepting, of course, mashed potatoes, my specialty, which is half potato and half butter.) And funny how things always end up tasting the same. Steak, pork chops, chicken, you can barely tell which animal it came from.

But the strange thing about it, we liked each other's food. If I didn't watch how she cooked it, the result was something I liked and ate with compliments. Though Kearney wasn't too much into cooking, I liked what she made, it was usually simple, wholesome, and tasted good.

The Red Jacket

I think you tend to a little more of my palate. Which is lucky for us, since, without your mother, you're still eating at my Truck Stop cafe. And as for the refinements of cooking, well, we both enjoy watching Martha Stewart. And of course, without your mother, salads may never darken our kitchen plates again.

The Gift of Dancing

Your mother and I never danced much. Though when we were young we might have danced a bit in our living room or bedroom, alone. We weren't really social people, going out for drinks and such at bars or clubs.

But I remember at one period in her life your mother got into the heavy aerobic dancing of Jazzercise. She'd go dressed in a dark blue leotard and tights and dance her heart out. I can see her now, blasting her legs back and forth, waving arms, smiling and laughing. She'd come home, her workout clothes soaked damper than a towel after a shower. She'd be happy and energized. She enjoyed the camaraderie of the other women dancing

The Red Jacket

there, too. All high-stepping their way to health through fast bopping rhythms and music.

And when you were very young, you began practicing ballet. You paid attention and worked hard at it, and I remember recitals where you were memorable characters: a carrot, a mouse, a soldier, a nutcracker with flashing sword.

And, of course, one of the great joys of my life was when you were the principal dancer of the Nutcracker, dancing Clara's part yourself. And I was in the ballet, too, Her Silberhaus, in my tuxedo and brightly-colored medals I made and pinned to my costume. I remember waving my hands as gracefully as I could to mime ushering the children around the stage, and graciously bending to hand out Christmas presents to costumed kids whose parents were watching from a full audience. And in this one production, it was my great glory to dance with you, young and accomplished in a white ruffled gown, and me in a tuxedo with a shiny stripe down the leg, as we waltzed the

The Red Jacket

party waltz, I playing the part of your father. It was a once-in-a-lifetime chance to dance with a ballerina, and it was great.

And I'd tried to convince your mother to dance with me in the production that year. So that the three of us would be on stage doing what you did best, pirouetting on point, with Her Silberhaus and Frau Silberhaus, your real mother and father, pointing and admiring from among the party crowd on stage. But Kearney wouldn't do it. You and I were ham enough to get up and perform on stage, because when you wanted to be the best at something, dancing before others was just part of being the best. And I was so immodestly proud of you that I accepted a part that needed to be played. It was fun. Really fun. The audience loved it.

And your mother, after watching us perform, sitting in the crowd as people admired you and wondered if the "Father" was a professional, your mother loved it, too. I remember her saying to you, "Oh, Claire, now I can die happy." And she meant she'd seen your beauty and your dancing and it had filled her up.

The Red Jacket

And now years later, after we've lost your mom, remember this about your dancing. It was a real gift you gave to her.

The Color Wheel

Your mother once had her colors done, which meant she went to a color specialist, a fashion consultant in bloom at the time, and was told whether she was a Summer, Fall, Spring, or Winter. Evidently one's beauty matched a season in life. And your mother was beautiful, with high round cheekbones and fine light hair, and eyes that were smiling and good weather. And I believe your mother was a Fall. I'm not sure.

Once you had your colors done, you were told certain things about your beauty and wardrobe. For example, Kearney was told she should not wear white, should wear her eye color —pleasant blue, when in meetings to put others into a relaxed receptive state, should not wear pointed designs in sweaters, jewelry, or blouses because rounds and curves were her gentle style. This all worked for me and seemed to work for her. And after shr heard all this, she was given a color wheel. A wheel that

The Red Jacket

fanned out in a circle of cloth swatches that showed the colors of your life and future clothes.

It freed Kearney to go into any store, holding her color wheel like a magnifying glass up to the clothes and determine if they were for her. If they were, she could buy something knowing without fear that it would match her other clothes. Kearney used her color wheel and I have to say, she was always a wonderfully put-together dresser. Her clothes were good, expensive, well cut, and the colors indeed went well with her. It freed her to accept new colors for herself.

Of course, it enslaved me, nearly preventing me from buying clothes as gifts. Unless I snuck out the color wheel to a Macy's or Nordstrom and stared at it and then to the desired sweater as if color-matching butterflies.

But you know, there were a lot of colors on that wheel. And I found I could pretty much get something beautiful, without points or zigzags, but with graceful curves, and it would match your mother. So, for her part, she made it easy. She was a person of many colors. And I could look around anywhere in the world and find them.

A Little Lesson

There was a time when I was doing lots of spiritual study, involving much assigned reading and daily meditations, and I was behind. The spiritual quest had become a labor in which I was like a man late for work chasing after a departing train. I seemed to be falling behind, getting smaller and smaller, as the train gained distance.

Kearney had already done this spiritual course a year or two before me. And completed it with ease. I asked her how she had time for it all. In truth, I wanted some sympathy for all this difficult work I was doing. And Kearney told me something that made it all easy. She told me that it was my study and that I should do it the way I wanted to do it. And that I should maybe do it in a way that was easy and pleasurable. If I thought I had to do a 45-minute meditation to fulfill the assignment, perhaps I could do the meditation in 5 to 15 minutes if that's all I had time to do. And this woke me up. My definitions were that I needed to do a lot of work to satisfy the assignments. But indeed all I needed to do was the amount that satisfied me. And if I redefined my spiritual work as pleasant and easy, it put a whole new light on what I was doing. It all seemed easy, and I returned to it with renewed energy, doing what satisfied me. The real goal was what I learned about myself, not whether a few hundred pages had been read in time for the next assignment.

And I'm not saying you should cheat on your homework, slide through stop signs, or let go of paying the bills. But I'm saying how you see your work has a lot to do with how you feel about it and how you do it. I think your mother was saying do what you can do, and enjoy it, and somehow the work will get done to your satisfaction. I'm sure our Puritan forefathers are rolling over in their graves. But if that's the work they want to do, let them. You can define your life as a success and it will be. And see, if I learned just this one little lesson from her in all this spiritual study, that was my success.

A White Mustang

Your mother liked to drive, especially small fast cars. When she was a teenager, her father bought the family, first, a small yellow Carmen Ghia, a kind of slouched beetle that you've probably never seen, and then the piece de resistance of the American small town, a white Ford Mustang.

These cars are kind of collector's items now, but Kearney drove one when it was just a car. She really liked the family Mustang. She liked to drive fast, she liked to shift and be in control, and I'm sure she had fun, hair flying as she tooled around the small town and country roads. It was a sporty roadster and she liked being in it.

For me it's a vision of freedom, a first freedom from family, that awakens in teenagers about that time. Kearney, a high-schooler, leaving home in a white Mustang, heading for wherever she wanted to head. I can easily imagine her driving with her friends and laughing. She liked driving, and she drove fast.

And for me, I see The Dream in it, a young girl in a white Mustang flying down an American country road.

Hawaii

Your mother loved Hawaii. There was something about the islands that really attracted her. Walking in loose clothes and sandals, hot weather everywhere, the incredible island beauty of palm trees leaning over clean blue and green waters, rising turtles, serpentine lava twisting over sand and rocks like an octopus, the verdant hills, sudden rain storms, people used to leisure between bouts of hard work, she found something there in herself that fed her.

So, being spiritual, your mother began studying Huna, a modernized version of ancient Hawaiian beliefs. She attended retreats and seminars and looked in depth at the meanings she saw. I remember when we visited, she enjoyed walks to sacred sights, pointing out hieroglyphs, the surfer, the turtle, the canoer, a bird, names of which I don't recall, but which had meaning to Kearney, seeing profound history carved into rocks. Surrounded by seeming paradise, ancient lore, foreign culture, spiritual boundaries and frontiers, she felt fully herself there. She felt light and at home. Amazed that a spot like that existed on earth. A paradise where she fit in. She found her Hawaii.

Moments in Oz

Sometimes kids see things with fresh eyes and intense clarity. And they are removed from childhood for a moment.

I remember it happened to me in a movie theatre, watching Steinbeck's "The Red Pony." I was seven or eight and not used to theatres. Many seats, kids milling and facing the screen in darkness. The movie had turned scary, a young horse was on its side laboring to breathe on a barn floor. It was raining and a boy was worried about his horse as the father looked worried. The father took out a pen knife to cut a hole in the horse's throat to breathe. And that scared me. I had to leave the theatre. I felt someone pulling out a knife to calmly cut a hole in my throat.

And your mom told me this happened to her. When she was little in a theatre she was watching "The Wizard of Oz." Now an old-time classic, it was still fairly new then. And Dorothy was treading cautiously through the darkened haunted forest, useless friends behind, spook-mist everywhere. And then battle, the Flying Monkeys are swooping down through the trees, screaming, legs running eerily. And all are surrounded in attack. A little girl, your mom climbed under her theatre seat and hid.

And I remembered Dorothy trapped and alone in the Witch's castle, staring into a crystal ball, at Auntie Em pleading to find her, when the Witch's cruel face appeared laughing at her. Oh, the fear and despair of the moment pierced me. I realized in shock that Dorothy was really alone.

So, let's remember compassion for those facing unfortunate or terrible truths. Seeing the worst with fresh eyes. Eyes that steal childhood from you. Truths that a kid's life and an adult's life are not so protected. Moments out of Oz. And we only have those three bumbling friends to get us through.

The Camolis

Some families have special words. In Kearney's family, when Paul was just a toddler, he would say a special word,

"Gocypa." And then everyone knew he wanted to go to the grocery store.

In our family, you invented the word "camolis." It means any car that is a convertible. And anytime Kearney was driving and she saw a convertible passing by, she would say, "Camolis!" And we all knew exactly what she meant. She was speaking to us in our own tongue.

The Red Jacket

In college, there was something special about your mother. It's hard to characterize, that something different about her, a liveliness, an awareness, a cheerful intelligence that was open to life. I can only allude to it by saying your mother often wore a red jacket.

It was a beautiful soft-leather jacket, fire-engine red, a worn suede, very comfortable looking. I believe a hand-me-down from her mother perhaps. Something Kearney had worn a lot; it was as relaxed on her as her own shadow. And it just bespoke something. Here's a person smiling and cheerful, with short hair, greeting you in a red coat and jeans. Something special happening right before your eyes.

The Red Jacket

She was all there, right in front of you, with a red jacket on.

I don't know where that red jacket went. I doubt Kearney would have thrown it out. It might be packed away in some closet or shelf somewhere. Waiting to be discovered about the house.

Of course, I believe if I were to find that jacket again, I'd cry.

Opportunities and Misunderstandings

There are a couple things in life that your mother regretted. They have to do with listening to others.

In college, your mother was a language major. She loved French, was studying Spanish and Russian. In her sophomore year, she wanted to apply for a foreign exchange scholarship, something that would take her overseas to study. She sought advice in a hallway from her foreign language counselor about getting into the program. The woman said something off-hand that it was very hard to get into the program. Kearney interpreted this as doubt, an aspersion, whether she would be accepted as a student. She didn't apply. That next year, no one had applied for the program and so no one went. Your mother really regretted that, listening to someone who didn't think and how it took a dream out of her life.

The Red Jacket

And somewhere during her schooling, Kearney would have liked to have become a newscaster. She was very up on political and current events, and she would have liked to be on camera and report the news.

But she didn't. Somewhere someone had told her that there weren't any women newscasters (at that time) so it would be very hard to get into the business. Of course, even five years later, out of college, you began to see women newscasters on every channel. Kearney felt disappointed that she'd listened. Again she'd not gone in the direction of a dream.

But there were many dreams your mother did pursue. Teaching overseas, getting an advanced linguistics degree, becoming a magazine editor for *PC* magazine, *PC World* magazine, becoming the Editor in Chief of *MacWorld* magazine, writing books, and having a child like you.

So, if a few dreams got away, I guess it's just the price she paid for listening to people who should have known better. She would tell you to pursue your dreams, don't entrust them to others.

A Short History

Here's a short history of what I know about your mom before you were born.

The Red Jacket

Kearney Jo Rietmann was born in The Dalles Oregon on December 21, 1950. She was a citizen of the U.S. and the city of St Gallen, Switzerland.

Your mother graduated from Kenniwick High School in 1969. It was a time when military representatives were showing up in schools in dress uniforms, complete with braids and service bars on their chests, including a new yellow bar with red

stripes, to explain military police actions and the domino theory of toppling Asian countries. It was a time when I first heard a neighbor talk of a relative's son killed by a mortar, so at least they didn't have to take it personally, as if some soldier had sighted and shot him. It was also a time when the first bloom of hippies was growing rapidly in San Francisco, and we kids were growing long hair and wearing funny clothes. I met your mother when she was a sophomore at Washington State University, Pullman, a cow college, in 1970.

The war was going full, veterans were returning from Viet Nam to go back to school, making difficult adjustments, finding

The Red Jacket

demonstrations against the things they fought for. I remember one or two telling me that in Viet Nam they'd never run so hard in their lives, and another was getting upset and shooting holes in the floor of his house.

Kearney was studious and beautiful. She first lived in a dorm, then moved in with dorm friends into a double-wide campus apartment trailer. Songs by John Denver and tunes like American Pie were popular. We spent most of our free time together.

Your mother graduated in 1973. I was living in Spokane, about 90 miles away from Pullman, writing poetry and working in a hotel.

Kearney and I got married March 24, 1974. We lived briefly in Spokane together, in a decrepit apartment in an old house that nearly burned down because of the cocaine addict who lived in the downstairs room. It was the kind of house that has an old couch sitting on the porch. But it was near a great park in Brown's Addition. We took many walks together. Kearney worked in a family friend's clothing store, Bumgartner's, and I

The Red Jacket

worked at the hotel. And your mother wanted to go into the Peace Corps, so we did.

At first we'd wanted to go to South America, because Kearney spoke Spanish and I knew a bit, too. But there were no places available. We were offered a place in Thailand. But we declined. Then we got a call that a new group was going to Morocco and we decided to go. The Peace Corps has a saying about its returning volunteers: Those that go to Asian countries come back peaceful, those that go to South America come back rebels, those that go to Africa come back crazy. We were off to Africa!

From 1974 to 1976 we lived in Morocco. It was a dry country with mud walls, and plenty of turbaned men and women in veils. A beautiful place, and terrible too. At one moment it was like living 75 years ago in a French colony, with strange hooked telephones and outdoor cafes. Then the next, you were living 300 years ago in an Arab medina with women carting live chickens by the legs, donkeys tottering by under huge piles of sticks, and a man with a goatskin under his arm offering to sell you water from a shiny cup that the whole medina has drunk from.

The Red Jacket

Your mother adjusted well, and because she spoke excellent French and was a superb language teacher, she was well respected in her school and our town. She had to learn to walk in a special way down the streets. She had to be nearly invisible, with a neutral face, or men and boys would bother her. However, she commanded respect with her great French, and she was good at living in Meknes, our little Moroccan sidewalk city. She had many Moroccan and French friends. She spoke Arabic in the medina. We had good times and bad times, in an exotic setting, palm trees in the sidewalks, the smell of orange blossoms and jasmine in the evening air. It was worth it.

We returned home in 1976 and landed in Los Angeles. Kearney had been accepted into the School of Linguistics at the University of Southern California. I applied there as well and was accepted into the masters program in education. So we found ourselves living in Hollywood for several years. Another whole new world like being in the Peace Corps, again a city with palm trees and all sorts of strange people. The first time we travelled across town, down the endless Western avenue to USC, we approached a stoplight just in time to have a police car slide to the curb in front of us. Two cops jumped out, guns drawn, and rushed into a corner liquor store. I

looked at the stoplight thinking, "Go green, go green."
Welcome back to America. We studied for two years in the endless smoggy summer of LA. In the winters the canyons filled with mud slides, in the summers San Bernadino burned down. We learned a lot about big cities, and crackling gunfire in the evening twilight.

Your Mother did well in grad school, and after that we took jobs at the University of Redlands in a special language teaching program run by a private organization. It was now around 1978. Kearney taught English language classes to Saudi Arabian students, generally older men who worked in the airline industry. They were always respectful and circumspect with your mother. We decided to go overseas again to make money. We had the degrees and we had the time.

So around 1979, we joined a company that represented a consortium of American universities that was setting up an Electricity and Electronics Institute (INELEC) in Algeria. We would teach English to young technicians and future engineers whose coursework was with American and Indian professors. The Algeria that we knew was green and lush, on the coast, with proud people who had fought and won a revolution against the French. It was a strong and brutal regime, police toting machine guns under their arms like women's purses. We set about living in a Russian-built compound of stiff, sterile three-story apartment buildings with water that ran once in the morning and once at night. Again Kearney was an excellent teacher, did well, and her students and colleagues respected her. We soon had Russian friends. There were 4000 Russians in the school compound, many teaching students in the textile industry. Our friends were probably party members, the privileged class of Russians. Our Russian friends were proud, honest, and strong. And man, they could drink vodka until you didn't know if your nose had fallen off. Good times and hard times again. Your mother was once sick, very sick, with what I believe was toxic shock. After several weeks she pulled through after losing the skin on her finger tips. Then I had a bad time. At the end of 16 months or so in the country, I fell ill to hepatitis. About 11 French kids and I came down with it, likely from contaminated water on the intermittent water system. It was a bad time, and Kearney did her best to take care of me. My face and skin turned pumpkin. It was probably isolating and hard, taking care of the sick in a foreign land. Kearney was strong and brave about it when she needed to be. And suddenly, we weren't young enough to be invulnerable anymore. It was time to go home.

We came home about 1981, landing in San Francisco. We joined a company as writers, writing English language lessons for ARAMCO, a Saudi Arabian oil company. We wrote lessons about things like turning on gas valves, reading recorders, and politely saying safety tips like, "Excuse me, Ahmed, I'm on

The Red Jacket

fire." Actually, we taught things like "Lift with your legs, not with your back." One of the most interesting things for Kearney was her discovery of a dedicated word-processing machine the company used, called a Vyadec, that looked a lot like a video arcade game, the kind you sit in for car racing. It was the first time Kearney or I had seen a word processor. We marveled at how efficient it would be for writers. We were sold. We bought a personal computer, brand new and a word-processing program. By the end of a year, Kearney had a job as an editor with MicroPro, a software company that was selling a red-hot product, WordStar, a word processor for the new IBM personal computers just being released. She just absorbed the software environment, again did well, became a publications manager in no time. I took a job at the Bank of America as a "Senior Educational" something. Our first real jobs outside of teaching.

Then Kearney took a job helping develop a product guide for *PC* magazine. The publishers loved her work. From probably 1983 to 1985, she held a series of ever more important jobs in the magazines, managing staffs of writers and other editors. She was sophisticated and knowledgeable about the whole software show. I remember her speaking to a group of 500 software developers at MacWorld once. She talked with and knew key industry people, the Peter Nortons, Dan Bricklins, the inventor of the first spreadsheet, VisiCalc, met Bill Gates,

Steve Jobs, and the founder of Lotus-1-2-3, people who eventually became multimillionaires. Kearney was at the very height of what she did best: learn things in depth and see an exciting future, applying her mind and doing good work.

And then in 1986, she had you. One triumph after another. (The heartaches, disappointments, the blues...we can look at those another day.) And you know, I knew Kearney for over 33 years. And it was just about enough time to get to know the important things about her.

A Small Thing Remembered Long

Once, late in the day in Morocco, we were home in our apartment and there wasn't much to eat. We were too tired to make the walk to the market and see what was edible.

So I made some rice and stirred in some tomato sauce, onion, something else. But it looked boring and thick, so I decided to see if I could spice it up a bit. I put in a dash of cinnamon, just to see.

That was the day I ruined my reputation as a chef. Kearney thought it was horrible. I did too.

She never let me forget it. And your mother had a long memory.

So, don't put cinnamon in the spaghetti sauce. Discerning palates like your mother's will know. And remember. For a long long time. To this day I can hear her say, "Well, at least I never put cinnamon in the...."

The Piñata

I'm painting a shining picture of your mother, I know. But no, she was not infallible.

Once when you were little, four or five, we decided to have a birthday party for you at our house, complete with piñata.

I'm leery of piñatas. They're usually made of something tough as elephant hide and difficult to break. You have to whack them like an old turtle and just hope they crack. Little kids are unlikely assailants.

But your mother had found a colorful example for the party. A donkey or something. Very crêpey with primary colors.

Being me, I had trepidations. I shook it before hanging it up for the party: Nothing. I said, "Kearney, I don't think there's any candy in this."

The Red Jacket

I received a forthright dismissal. They always put candy in the piñata.

Hoist of shoulders in reluctant acceptance. The donkey piñata is strung up, a dangling party victim.

Parents and kids enter, lots of kids running everywhere. Wind devils let loose in the party house.

Time for the piñata! Stick handed out. Kids swinging and bashing to no effect. Just a swinging donkey thunking happily along. Finally, I believe I reach and break it open so the kids can finally belly flop onto the goodies as they hit the kitchen linoleum.

Nothing. The piñata is empty.

Kearney flushes red —and we move on to the next event.

And I think the moral of the story is: never buy anything that you're going to have to beat with a stick to make work.

The Red Jacket

When You Were Born

Your mother prepared and had me prepare for your birth. We took Lamaze classes at the local hospital, breathing in and out through crisis, and watched films of births that I guess brutalized you enough to accept a difficult process as under control. One memorable film showed a woman on her back in labor, her husband bending to attend to her pain, and getting slapped hard in the face. Pop! I remembered that. And no purple hearts were awarded.

Oddly, Kearney had a close friend, Carol, who was pregnant as well. Both had nearly the same due dates. The evening of your birth Kearney was on the phone to Carol discussing baby progress, Braxton Hicks contractions, and such. Suddenly Kearney realized she'd wet her pants. She got off the phone and said to me wasn't that funny. I said, "Grown people don't wet their pants." She knew her water had broken. So we called the doctor, were told to head for the hospital.

The Red Jacket

Oddly, when we were safely stored in one of the birthrooms, we find out Carol and her husband have just arrived. Both babies were born that night. So you were born with a friend. This should probably become standard clinical practice.

So, the details of the birth (as much as you, the birthee, can

probably stand): Your mother was calm in labor, things went slowly but okay, measurements taken, contractions timed, I was there helping her focus through the pain. Cheerful nurses strode in and out checking progress. Finally it was time. Our doctor, Dr. Prinze, was a calm and confident man. He strode in in green, helped out, checked things, finally took a green cloth bundle, a medical parachute pack, and unwrapped all his tools. He snips and pulls and there you are. He tells me to cut the umbilical cord, which I'd told him I wasn't going to do, and I cut it. You're born, you're in your mother's arms, you're safe, and your mother is fine.

A miracle.

The Red Jacket

Her Piano

It's a black piano. It came with her through her childhood. She learned to play simple music and chords, church music, and a few tunes. Your mother loved singing, but never went far to develop her skills on the piano. I think she was content with where she was. She would sit at the piano, open the church hymnal, and play the old ones she knew. Simple hymns, walking chords, harmony without embellishment. The church music she knew.

She never practiced. She simply opened the book and read the chords and fingerings she'd learned in childhood. A simple music remembered. It sustained her.

It's a heavy old black piano. I know, I've hefted it from one house to another. Like carrying your whole childhood on your back. Your mother would sit at it and play it. The old church hymns. It sustained her.

The Red Jacket

Each of us has a black piano that we play. It comes in different shapes and sizes. The softball diamond that you play on. The books I write. You play it the way you like it. And it sustains you.

Smaller Than a Bread Box

Here's a mystery about your mother that I could never figure out. She didn't like small animals around her. Small pet birds, especially. There was something there that she'd rather not be around. She grew to love Gypsy our cat, but she didn't like smaller creatures. I questioned her on this once. What about a big dog like Ferd (John Lewis' hulking black Labrador.) No problem. What about a raccoon? She wasn't so sure about a raccoon. I worked down on the size of the animals I asked her about until it appeared anything under the size of a bread box was suspect. Something about irrational blinky-eyed birds she really didn't trust. I never learned what made this so.

The Red Jacket

A Horror Tale

Your mother once told me a horror tale from her childhood. Two families, hers and another business acquaintance family, would do weekend holidays on The River. This meant taking a family ski-boat down to the Columbia, finding a sandy river bank or dock at a park, and spending a day of picnicking, drinking, and water-skiing. Kearney's family enjoyed skiing, and I believe your mother at 10 or 12 was a good water skier, slaloming on a single ski behind a fast boat.

The other family, the Rutherfords, I believe, were part of the skiing party. They had a son maybe Kearney's age at the time, perhaps another boy or girl as well. The details don't serve me well.

And Kearney told me on this weekend, the other family's mother was going to ski. The boat took off. But the rope was wrapped around her hand. It caught her by surprise and wrenched off a finger.

Panic for everyone. The holiday families erupt with an emergency and bleeding. And Kearney said the son was told

The Red Jacket

to go dive into the water and find his mother's finger. And so he did. And Kearney remembered him diving into the water, and diving and diving. A serious and heroic effort. Finding nothing.

Kearney remembered this. Twenty, thirty years later, she remembered.

And why? Why did that happen? All I can say is that sometimes life puts you in those situations. Where you have to dive into murky waters looking for things you're perhaps afraid to find.

Hold your breath and go. Do your best. Just get through.

Pup

You probably don't know this, but your mother's family had a dog when I first met them. It was a small black dachshund, black pointy face, salami body, a tail that whipped for attention like a conductor's wand. Its name was Pup.

I don't remember much about it, except the family didn't seem to like it much. Skepticism floated over this animal as it walked between leather chairs, new couches, indoor carpeting. It was kind of a four-legged criminal. The usual suspect.

Years later, you and I would take care of a similar dog for our friends, the Wagners. This dog was so old, it could barely walk, shaking and trembling as if it just stepped out of a refrigerator. You and I nicknamed it "Shivers." And we tried to get it outside for a walk whenever the neighbors left it in our company during vacations. It would stand as if mesmerized by the expanse of the small lawn, blinking and cheerful feeling real sunlight, seeing green to walk on. This seemed to perk up the old bologna.

Shivers lived nearly forever, as long as a dog could possibly survive in a low-shaking tube for a body. Our neighbor, Cathy, was upset when Shivers died.

Pup somehow just blipped off the radar. I've no clue how or when that dog went to the eternal dog-salami resting ground. But, I think Shivers was the luckier dog.

The Snail

Your mother paid attention to the phases of your growing up. I remember one phase we watched: Baby puts everything in mouth. Kearney would take you to the beach, all the glittering pebbles at the water's edge: These were quite a mouthful. She'd let you crawl and toddle, picking up and tasting the ocean gems. She told me it was a phase that would pass. It did.

But not before one memorable day. You were out in the back patio, walking the way little kids do, as if your legs were a wishbone with shoes. And Kearney called me, you'd found a snail. And when I came out, you were holding the snail in your mouth like a very short cigar.

Glad your mom and I made it through that phase. I wouldn't have survived a rainy day with angle worms on the sidewalk.

Halloween Mother

It was the first Halloween where you knew the fun of dressing up. You were three or so. Your mom had you costumed as a fairy princess, complete with wings and a garland of flowers in your hair. You were running around excited. It was getting dark.

A knock at the door. You ran to it and pulled it open to see.

There stood a teenager in a bloody army uniform. He looked like he'd been shot out of a cannon and the mangled body had landed standing on our doorstep.

You turned and ran for your mother.

You were a fairy princess in your mother's arms for a good long while.

Eating Together

Remember sitting around the table the three of us eating together? Probably not. We never did. We were one of those American families that cooks and moves food directly from the kitchen into the family room. We ate from plates in our laps, on the floor, on wooden TV trays. You ate as you did homework, I as I watched TV, your mother as she read her book or newspaper on the couch.

Gypsy, our long-haired Persian cat, would walk through waiting to see if anyone would pay attention to her. If I was reading a newspaper on the floor, she'd lie down in the middle of page 2, waiting to see if I dared move her.

For dinner, I would cook you and I some heavier dish. A pasta or meat of some sort or beef teriyaki with rice. Your mother generally ate something lighter, a salad, a baked potato. Sometimes a little of what we were having. And often tea of herbal brew.

I guess I wouldn't say we ate together, because we never as a family surrounded a dinner table and ate our table-captured food. But we ate together each night, on couches, floor, trays.

Comfortably, like the way you see apes eat in their zoo exhibits, as we watched TV and paid little interest to what was going on in the rest of the zoo.

Decorating the Tree

So here's the way your mother, you, and I decorated the Christmas tree.

You and I work the beast into a stand, screwing it tight, so that it's supposed to stand up.

We haul it like a dead man into our living room, and stand it up, hoping the dead man won't lean and fall over.

I string the little twinkle lights around the tree as you and your mother pick out ornaments, one by one placing them like jewels or Easter eggs in the branches. You find all the right spots. The little glass bells find a special place.

I put a few ornaments in the last top branches. Now the tree is fully loaded.

We stand back to admire. And because we've basically put all the ornaments on one side of the tree, the tree falls over.

The Red Jacket

Titles

Here are a few books your mother read in the last year or so of her life:

A Course in Miracles, Foundation of Inner Peace

A Simple Path, the Dalai Lama

Bone, Dying into Life, Marion Woodman

Care of the Soul, Thomas Moore

Teach Only Love, Gerald Jampolsky

The Power of Now, Eckhart Tolle

Forgiveness, Neale Donald Walsch

Questions for Someday

Someday you might ask:

Did I love my mother enough?

You did.

Was I a good daughter to my mother?

Oh yes, outstanding.

Did she love me, her daughter, Claire?

Clearly. The one grand certainty for me. She was there to the end for you.

Did my mother have a good life?

Yes, better than most, good as any.

What happened that she had to leave us? Why did this happen?

We don't know, you were never the cause, you worked against the impossible.

Did I do my best as we walked my mother through the crisis, the ordeals, the operation, the stress and pain of hospitals?

You did, you did.

Someday, when Spring comes and the feelings thaw: you had the right answers.

Being on Top of Things

Your mother played a role of being on top of her life, managing all well. People respected her for it, but it also protected her. No one saw her mistakes, it guarded her privacy, she kept prying eyes out. She was "on top of things." And I realize now, being on top of things doesn't always give you rest. When she took on a new job, a new challenge, met new people, she took it on as mastering a task. She put herself deeply into it, looking ahead, getting on top of it, figuring it out. It was a successful strategy in her life. But behind the strategy, it also may have made her feel a bit alone. And it was tiring.

Things We Won't Know

There are things we won't know that we must mourn.

What your mother would have said on your high school graduation.

What your mother would have said on winning the softball championship.

What she would have said upon your graduating college.

What she would have said upon your getting married.

At a certain point in her illness, I'd hoped that she'd write letters to say these things to you later in your life. But she didn't write them. She had no intention of not being there, she was going to say them to you directly.

We didn't know.

The Red Jacket

Years From Now

Someday you will look back and try to remember things about your mother. And it all may seem kind of distant.

And I can imagine that will be a terrible thing. Such an important part of yourself somehow distanced.

But, if you look closely around you, I think you'll see reminders all the time. A mother clapping for a kid dancing ballet, a happy skeptical laugh, someone slouching on a couch reading intensely. There will be moments when you see her.

Walking along oceanside cliffs, someone merrily waving in the distance, someone picking at a baked potato with a fork, someone with a crooked pinky finger, someone with a genuine smile. You'll see her if you look.

Watch out for honest blue eyes crinkling happy to see you. Someone with a pointed-up nose, someone with fine light hair and sea-shell ears, someone who says they only shop at Nordstrom, never at Target. Watch out for a person sitting on a couch tending a very precious bowl of popcorn in her lap. You'll see these and remember her.

And, if you really need to see her, remember yourself as a kid, look in the mirror, look back, look in your own face. She's there in your kid laugh, in the color of your hair, she's there in your aspirations to excel, she's there in that crooked pinky finger, she's there, Babe. She's there.

The Sun

Studying the Hawaiian way of Huna, your mother told me of something she did. She often, daily, meditated throughout the last third of her life. And in Huna, she said, you could visualize the things that were bothering you, things that hurt, that worried, and give them away. You meditated and visualized sending them off, farewell, into the eye of the Sun. And it left you freer to see your life, solve your problems. Kind of gives our star so far away and untouchable a nice usefulness. The Sun, a spiritual aid that shines down all day. So let's take Kearney's advice and as we tug with pains we never imagined we'd have, let's send off those we can to the heart of the Sun. Let it carry that heavy weight for us. Your mother pointed the way.

A Detail

Funny how our lives are packed in between the details. So here is a detail about your mom. She ate carefully washed salads, green lettuce, a few cubes of cucumber, nothing fancy. She would buy butter lettuce and wash it thoroughly. Then with a paper towel spread on the counter, she'd dismantle the entire head and lay out all the leaves like surgical equipment. She'd dry them off, putting a paper towel over the leaves and patting. Then she'd gather her leafy eats and put them in a pink bubble gum-color tupperware bowl sealed with a milky translucent lid. This would go in the refrigerator or be carted off to work for a lunch she picked at on her desk. There's a lot of people in the world who don't receive as much attention as those heads of butter lettuce.

The Picture of Your Mother

Here's a picture of your mother we'll always remember.

It's a self-portrait that your mom created from a photo she scanned. Then she applied different software effects to see how they worked. She was just playing around. One of the effects she liked was applying the water reflection in the background. And the changing of a photo to a watercolor. Suddenly she just stopped and she liked what she'd created.

The Red Jacket

It's a wonderful picture of her. Unexpected art capturing unspoken things about your mom.

I've kept it because it was important. As important as any piece of art ever made. Imagine, a masterpiece your mom made without intention. A stumbled-upon masterpiece.

What do you see, Claire? Because when I look at Kearney's face, her thoughtful eyes, I see a lot. I see a lot.

Your Name

Your mother named you Claire. You get this name from a dear friend of your mother's that we met in Morocco. She was a French teacher working in a Meknes. Claire and your mother worked in the same Lycee and became great friends.

The Red Jacket

Claire Imanatoff was a young Parisian, in her twenties, in a teenager's body, short, curly black hair, glasses, and mignon look. She was intelligent and feeling, and candid in a French way. She lived in a small villa with her boyfriend Daniel and her two young boys, ages 2 and 4. They had nicknames of Manu and Cici.

Claire was an English teacher like Kearney and she spoke it well. Kearney spoke English or French with her depending on who else was listening and needed to be included.

When Claire was young, she was a bit rebellious. She lived in central Paris and her parents were strict, forbid her to go out on the town at night. In her teens, she'd sneak out the window. I remember her telling us how she'd gone out and made love for the first time with her boyfriend one night. Then she became pregnant just like that. She said it wasn't true that you couldn't become pregnant if it was your very first time!

After that things were hard. Her boyfriend split and there were few jobs. She ended up coming to Morocco for work. She was a bit adventurous and very bright. Your mother enjoyed her, I think because they had the same bright minds. I think your mother saw an independence that she liked. Claire was living her own life and taking care of things. And your mother shared this independent outlook on life. Daily they faced the same trials in the classroom, in the taxis, in the market, in the streets of being foreign women in an Arab land. And yet Claire was brave, caring, and had a good outlook.

So, when you were born, and we were thinking up names, it was no accident that Kearney thought of her friend and named you Claire. The idea of that name had a lot of good things behind it.

An Admirable Thing About the Rietmanns

So you know who you are, you should know an admirable thing about your mom's family. Your mom was proud of Uncle Van and his family with their roots in wheat farming and ranching. They live 20 miles from the nearest small town of Condon, Oregon, small enough that a stray cat can cross it in about ten minutes walking slow. And a guard dog at the service station may or may not look up.

It's wheat country. You see yellow combines roving over the rolling hills like miniature vacuum cleaners. Trucks pull up. Wheat pours into a hill in the back beds. Dust kicks up ghostly behind the trucks hauling yellow loads away toward farm silos.

Van and his family are farm folks with a difference. They know their business deeply and farm on the cutting edge. And they

The Red Jacket

try to see beyond. It's the kind of farm with an airplane that the son Tom flies to Spokane for parts. You see a satellite dish beside the house used to check the daily grain prices as far away as Tokyo. They plant experimental crops and measure careful statistics about fertilizers and yields, and are quick to determine what works and what's useless. They look ahead and try to stay on the leading edge. I remember Uncle Van telling me as we looked out across fallow hay-strewn acres that their type of dry-land farming wasn't sustainable. It was destroying the topsoil. He was talking decades from now. Van was making a hard description of his efforts long term, what farming meant, appraising the real problem. He said if I had any answers he'd welcome them. A man concerned with the real issue of saving the earth. And Kearney was proud of them.

Proud of Van, Rosie, her cousin Tom and his wife Katie who work there. They farm but with a difference. Their work is on the farm but their hearts are in the world. They have a world outlook that is uncommon. Their daughter, Ann Marie, had left the farm to become first an intern in Washington D.C., then an active political campaigner, later a lobbyist. When the U.S. was setting up to fight insurgents in Nicaragua, the Rietmanns were concerned and travelled there to see farm programs and know what was happening to the people. They are concerned with peace initiatives. And they are troubled by our often aggressive government. These Rietmanns are not back road farmers, they have a vision that goes beyond their fields, their county, out across their nation and into the globe beyond. They live with intelligence and involvement, have values that they think are important, and your mom was proud of them. They are Rietmanns with an admirable difference.

And, if you're a little kid visiting their farm, they'll make sure you ride the horse.

Today You Cried

You cried because it was unfair. You'd found a passage in your religion class that talked about taking "baby steps" to get where you need to go. You remembered this was a part of your mom's favorite movie, "What About Bob?" A funny movie in which Bill Murray is a goofy neurotic playing to Richard Dreyfuss' uptight psychiatrist. The psychiatrist had written a book called "Baby Steps" to help his clients heal and to help himself into national fame. Bill Murray is grab-your-stomach-and-roll funny and your mom used to yodel with glee to watch him. There's one scene where he's tied himself to a sailboat mast and he's screaming I'm sailing! I'm sailing! in triumph over his fear of sailing. He's wrapped in ropes like a mummy.

You wanted to come home and share this funny find in your religion book with your mother. But you realized she wasn't there, and never would be. And it was unfair and you were angry. And you cried.

And, Claire, each time we cry that way, it's baby steps.

Compassion

Your mother once took a trip to France. It was the summer of her sophomore year in college and she'd signed up to go to Pau to study. It was a big deal for her, from the Tri-Cities and wheat country, to go to France on her own. She'd never been. She didn't know anyone there, she went alone. It must have taken some grit to decide to go and to get on the plane, armed only with a big heavy suitcase and American-learned French.

When she landed in Paris, I guess things were confusing. She was alone with a heavy suitcase, new to everything, and unsure. I believe she was getting herself to a hotel, but felt lost and worried. She was having trouble lugging this too-heavy suitcase around, so she couldn't really explore for information. She had an anchor tied to her. It was difficult even limping across a busy street. She said that she got to a certain point where she didn't know where to go and couldn't go any further. Lost in a foreign land with the unseeing natives walking by briskly. I guess she asked a young man for help and he wasn't sure what she wanted. He didn't understand. Then your mother cried. And the young man stopped and saw

The Red Jacket

your mother. He helped your mom with her suitcase and took her to her hotel. Your mother needed help and someone was good enough to see and give it.

I hope someday to have compassion like that. To see, understand, and do the right thing. And thereafter, your mother felt better about being in France, and she had a great summer traveling and making friends. A little bit of compassion goes a long way. All the way across the ocean back to us.

Notebooks

Around in our closets and drawers, I bet we have a hundred notebooks, wire bound, filled with notes on carefully lined green paper. As your mother lived, she wrote to herself. All sorts of things. Feelings, thoughts, dreams, passages of this and that. She filled up many cahiers. You find them spread like lily pads beside her bed, like stepping stones around her desk. Like plates of pancakes beside her computer, under her chair.

I glanced through them from time to time. I always hoped she was writing something for us, to be published, to show others. But these notes were personal and only for her. They don't add up enough that I can compile them together and give them to you, saying, "Here, a book from your mother."

She wrote things just for herself. No intention of furthering anything about herself or her career or publishing. It's a dialogue of her inner conversation with herself, of her thoughts, about things around her. There is absolutely no promotion in it. A completely honest stream of writing. And though they don't add up, I will keep these books for you for as long as you may need them, the books of your mother's life. Someday, when you have the heart to read them, they may add up to a lot for you.

Couscous

Your mother and I lived in Morocco for three years. And strange, though you've never been, one of the dishes you like to eat is couscous. First we make a kind of vegetable stew with cabbage, carrots, onions, olives, turnips, chick peas, and Moroccan spices, cumin, pepper, cinnamon, cilantro, lemon. Your mother liked it with just vegetables. You and I liked it with a little chicken. You put the stew over the couscous. A big white mound of couscous. Then you dig in with a spoon.

Your mother liked cooking it. It fills the house with a sweet savory cooking smell. And the couscous itself is easy to cook: boil water, put in an equal amount of couscous. Let sit. The couscous rises white and thick, like dough. Drain, serve piled in a bowl.

The Red Jacket

Of course, the way we cooked and ate it is nothing like the way Moroccans do. You couldn't know. But real Moroccan couscous is steamed. It's fairly moist, thick, and sticky when done, and you eat it by taking your right hand and rolling some couscous into a ball the size of a doughnut hole and popping it in your mouth.

Your mother and I liked learning to cook and eat couscous in Morocco. So we brought it home to the States. And now you like it. And though I tried to teach you some of the funny words we know in Arabic, (for example the word for "nothing" is "walu," and the word for couscous is "suksu") it's your mother's couscous that stuck. You're an American girl who likes couscous. A part of your mother come to you from her travels in a mysterious African land.

And by the way, your mother spoke Moroccan Arabic. Enough to tell you the joke about the man in the medina who points to the sky and asks in Arabic, "Is that the sun or the moon?" and the other man, also an idiot, who answers and shrugs, "I don't know, I'm not from here."

"Wesh hadi l'shimps ou l'gmara?"

"Mnarf, ana mashi min hna."

Tarot Cards

Your mother could read Tarot cards. I know that seems like a very "California" thing to do, but your mother had deeply schooled herself in the meanings of the Kabbala and its relationship with the cards. She could turn over a card, look at its peculiar symbolism, the Hanged Man dangling upside down in the shape of a four, the impishly smiling Devil with the chained lovers before him, the fearful falling Tower, and tell you about a piece of yourself. And people listened and came away convinced. Convinced that they'd heard about themselves, their futures, their inner hearts. Your mother was intuitive, clear sighted, and when she explained the meanings of the cards to listeners, they came away feeling they'd been seen, heard, understood. And then people apply their own magical thinking to such things and imagine someone is predicting the future. Not so, your mom had really just told them the truths of things that went on inside them. And, of course, (a secret of the cards) that's what creates the future.

The Red Jacket

Makeup

Your mother didn't wear much makeup. A little light facial powder to smooth her cheeks, a little mascara. No perfumes, no lipstick. On the most formal occasions, a bit of eye shadow. She had makeup kits, lipsticks, and those curious curved pincers that curl eyelashes, like little rubber eyelid guillotines. But these mostly went unused. Your mother had a beautiful shapely face, and it didn't take much to make her look good. She used shampoos and hair conditioners for light fine hair. She used cold cream to remove eye shadow and mascara, but never anything with aloe. She was allergic to aloe, and anything that was applied to her face with aloe in it had horrific results. She'd be forced to wear sunglasses for a week until her puffed eyelids subsided. It made her look like a movie star hiding her fame behind sunglasses worn indoors.

The Red Jacket

Church

Your mother came from a church-going family. And the church was an important and sustaining part of her family as she grew up. Her parent's interest moved from business, to politics, to church and spiritual work.

David, Kearney's dad, studied deeply to become an Episcopal deacon, and spent years in white robes serving others. He was not much of a preacher, slow-spoken and affable, but he was strong in service. He went to help the elderly at old folks homes daily, conducted prayers, helped people in real ways. Kearney grew up singing in the choir with her mom and sister. Her mom was a church leader and to this day holds church classes in her home. Paul, Kearney's brother, took on the church as a vocation, became an Episcopal priest whom his congregation looks up to and enjoys. Kris, Kearney's sister, is deeply involved with strong religious values for her family and sons. It was in the family. Kearney knew the liturgy, services, holy days, the books of prayer, the hymns. She knew overweight priests who sweated as they preached, strange priests who prayed in tongues at the dinner table, and the honorable Bishop Swing, the Bishop of California, who visited

The Red Jacket

our home on several occasions. It was a childhood part of her that she kept. Even when her broad education in psychology, philosophy, metaphysics, mythology, and spiritual studies led her to new things, she still attended church and was a part of that Sunday morning meeting group. And though you and I aren't much into church, I like to think that for Kearney church was a good reason to get up on a beautiful sunny morning and see old friends.

Gifts

Your mother knew how to accept gifts. The happy surprise and the thank yous. A balance of grace and acceptance. You and I were often unsure about what to get your mom for Christmas, her birthday. We'd wander stores and do our best. And sometimes we did good. I remember once you and I bought her a sophisticated green bracelet from a jewelry store, and a deep blue one, too. And I remember she'd wear the green one with a Kelly green sweater to formal occasions and meetings. And I once bought her a watch with different colored stones on a linked gold bracelet, curving intertwined metals, and she liked that and wore it. And we bought her a bracelet from The Museum Store that had colored scarabs on it, pretty, and she wore that to work. These were gifts we gave and did good.

And, of course, we did good when we gave your mother her last surprise birthday party. Everyone came. It was a big party. And it was the last time she truly felt safe and happy. We did good.

Never Cried

When your mother found out she had cancer, a brain tumor, and we went through a long losing ordeal, she never cried. She never complained or asked, "why me?" She simply summoned her courage and did what she could to survive. She learned and she did what she could. She asked questions. She remained positive. Cheerful. And she never cried.

Of course, you and I cried, a good deal.

The Art of Conversation

If the phone rang at ten o'clock it would be a friend calling up to talk with your mother. Your mother knew how to talk. She was lively, and she'd suddenly throw back her head and laugh

The Red Jacket

as she listened. She would gush amusement. Her brow would scrub up with concern. The person in front of her felt listened to, felt heard. She had broad interests and knew the detail beyond the norm, and so could talk with just about anyone about their world. She knew how to do it. People liked talking with her.

I think she learned a little of it from her father in the shoe store. You talk and are easy with people as you show them new shoes. You put them at ease. You serve with pleasantries. Her father was good at it. Kearney learned a thing or two in the store.

And she taught me a secret of conversation. When you're not sure you have anything to say, just ask questions. And listen to the answers. If you put your mind to the answers, you'll see the person and connect. You can ask questions that stir the other person to think. Ask real questions and eventually you'll know who you're with. He or she will see you want to know them. They'll be pleased. Then, like your mother, talk to your heart's content.

The Look

Your mother would sometimes pull her mouth to the side. It was a look of quizzical perplexity. Something happened, she dropped a spoon deep down the garbage disposal, the ice

The Red Jacket

cream ball rolled off her cone and fell on the floor— and your mother's mouth pulled sideways. It was not really a grimace, because only half her mouth pulled sideways. So I guess you could call it a "grim." But that sounds too negative, it doesn't capture the comical part of the look, a childlike "huh?" So I guess I would call that look a "grunk." Gypsy the cat jumps into your mother's lap as she's trying to read the newspaper and your mom stares down with a little grunk on her face. The grunk of friendly perplexity.

I don't have a picture of Kearney doing a grunk. But here's your version.

The Red Jacket

Ready to Serve

As you and I are moving on, I realize one thing about your mother now after she's left us. She was not worried about you or me. She saw clearly and knew we'd get through. She knew us.

If you think about it, it's kind of a gift that she didn't have to worry about you. I think she knew that you were done, "cooked" as she sometimes put it. The ingredients had been put in, the dough kneaded, the bread baked. And when the bread comes out, that's the way it is. It's done, cooked. You can't really change it.

She didn't have to worry about you. You are headed in the right direction, you're caring, you have a sense of good values, fairness, respect, and esteem for yourself. Unlike other teenagers who are perhaps lost, hurt, experimenting with dangerous parts of life, or perhaps angry and aimed at hurting, others heading for trouble, not seeing the long-term results of their daily vision, kids with real problems, you are in good shape. You have goals, determination, things you want to do. She saw your

The Red Jacket

courage and your good mind, and your incredible perseverance. Your strength for good. No, she didn't worry about you.

That's not to say you won't have your challenges. You'll face problems, need to grow, make mistakes, need to forgive yourself and others. You'll have to find new values that fit the circumstances of your life. You'll have to choose what's good for you over what others think. So, welcome to life. But Kearney knew your foundation was there. She knew who you were and she didn't worry. She tried to communicate a bit of who she was to you, so you'd have that. But she wasn't worried about you. You were done. Cooked. Ready to serve.

www.ingramcontent.com/pod-product-compliance
Lightning Source LLC
Chambersburg PA
CBHW042332150426
43194CB00001B/27